LORD Forgive Me

**PRAYERS OF CONFESSION
CYCLE B**

DAVID L. WADE

LORD, FORGIVE ME

Copyright 1987 by
The C.S.S. Publishing Company, Inc.
Lima, Ohio

All rights reserved. No part of this publication may be reproduced, stored in a retrieval system, or transmitted in any form or by any means, electronic, mechanical, photocopying, recording, or otherwise, without the prior permission of the publisher. Inquiries should be addressed to: The C.S.S. Publishing Company, Inc., **628 South Main Street, Lima, Ohio 45804.**

7871 / ISBN 0-89536-885-4   PRINTED IN U.S.A.

Table of Contents

Preface	5
Acknowledgments	6
Suggestions for Use	7

The Advent Season — 9

The Christmas Season — 13

The Epiphany Season — 18

The Lenten Season — 28

The Easter Season — 38

Calendar index for the Sundays after Pentecost Sunday — 49

The Sundays after The Day of Pentecost — 51

Special Days

Christmas Eve/Day	13
New Year's Eve/Day	14
Holy Name of Jesus	16
The Baptism of Our Lord	19
The Transfiguration of Our Lord	27
Ash Wednesday	28
Sunday of the Passion	34
Palm Sunday	35
Maundy Thursday	36
Good Friday	37
The Resurrection of Our Lord	38
Ascension Day/Sunday	44
The Day of Pentecost	46
The Holy Trinity	47, 48
Christ the King	77
Reformation Sunday	78
All Saints' Sunday/All Saints' Day	79
Thanksgiving Eve/Day	80

Preface

As a campus minister (United Ministries at Ball State University) during the 1970s, I was impressed by the work of a Lutheran colleague, Roger Sasse (Center for University Ministries at Indiana University), especially in the area of worship. He created a new service for each week, after reflecting with other participants on the proposed theme and Scripture lessons for the service, including each week what he referred to as a "Call to Honesty." For several years, and with his permission, I *borrowed* his writings for use in worship with students. Eventually, I began to create my own prayers of Confession, related to the Scripture lessons and worship theme for the day. These efforts met with success among the United Ministries student community, and on my return to parish ministry in 1982, I continued the practice of writing prayers of Confession in contemporary style and language.

This first selection follows the Common, Lutheran, and Roman Catholic Lectionaries for Cycle B. If they are successful, prayers for Cycle C and A will follow in order. I offer them as worship aids to congregations and pastors who would like to try something a bit more contemporary in their worship life, and as aids to personal devotion for individuals.

> David L. Wade
> Rock Springs, Wyoming
> May 1, 1986

Acknowledgments

Thanks to:

Jean Wade, for her constant support and encouragement to "be creative";
Kathy Smith, for her efforts in deciphering my writing and typing the manuscript;
the students of United Ministries at Ball State University, Muncie, Indiana; and the members of First Congregational Church, United Church of Christ, Rock Springs, Wyoming for their acceptance and encouragement of creative worship life.

Suggestions for Use

These Prayers of Confession were written for and used in corporate worship at the First Congregational Church, United Church of Christ in Rock Springs, Wyoming. They are written in the first person, to be read by the congregation in unison, following a pastoral Call to Confession, and followed by both Pastoral and Congregational Assurances of pardon. The intent of the first-person style is to affirm that, as we gather for worship, we are both individual seekers and believers and also the Body of Christ. Our sins and failings are our own, but they are also universally human. The first-person style makes it more difficult for us to say "They needed that" or "That doesn't apply to me"! It is much easier for us to "cop out" when reading or hearing a traditional, general Prayer of Confession.

As with any creative effort, the prayers vary in many ways, not only from traditional Confessions, but from each other. They may focus on the primary theme of the Scripture passage — the Gospel for the day — or they may pick up on a secondary or even tertiary theme. In a few cases, the focus is on the day itself, rather than the actual words of Scripture.

The personal style, while intended for use by a corporate, worshiping community, does open them up to different kinds of usage. Some possibilities might include: personal preparation for corporate worship through printing in Sunday worship folders, or "in advance" through inclusion in weekly bulletins or newsletters; as a focus for lectionary study groups or in sermon or homily preparation; as an aid to personal devotions; or in other ways that you might devise to suit your own congregation or situation.

Regardless of the way in which you might choose to use them, my hope is that you will find them meaningful in your life and ministry.

Advent 1

Matthew 13:32-37

Advent means Coming!
    The coming of Christ to the world;
    The coming of God to aid,
        To comfort,
                To judge?
Advent means anticipation!
    The growing light of the candles,
    The growing excitement of the season,
    The nearness of Christ.
Advent means anxiety!
    The connection with Apocalypse,
        The Second Coming,
        God's judgment on the world,
                          On me!
But what is "coming" for me
                Is Santa Claus!
    What I anticipate
               Is fun,
                  Gifts,
                  Parties!
    What makes me anxious
        Is gift selection,
            Delivery schedules
                  — January bills!
Lord, forgive me for secularizing your celebration,
        For dwelling on the social side of Christmas;
    And help me to see the Christ in Christmas
                  And the Christ in me.
    In his name I ask it.
                Amen

Advent 2

Mark 1:1-8

"Are you ready for Christmas?"
    A familiar question —
      A foolish question!
          With predictable answers!
  Kids are *always* ready
        — 365 (or 66) days a year!
  Adults are *never* ready;
      I always need more time to prepare,
         To shop,
         To bake,
         To clean,
         To decorate.
    Christmas catches me unprepared;
      It sneaks up on me!
  "Only sixteen more days? You're kidding!"
And I'm as unprepared for the coming of Christ
    As I am for Christmas!
      I haven't dusted the corners of my heart!
I have cobwebs on my soul!
My spirit is a trash heap!
I *want* to be ready!
  I *try* to be ready!
    But I'm *not* ready!
O Lord, forgive my unreadiness to receive you,
    To welcome you into my life
  As a Babe — or as Lord.
And teach me to invite you in, anyway,
    Secure in your acceptance of me
    Just as I am.
        For Jesus' sake.
        Amen

Advent 3

John 1:6-8, 19-28

"Who are you?"
>That's what they asked John.
>>"Are you the Christ?"
>>"Are you Elijah?"
>>"Are you the prophet?"
>No, I am a messenger,
>>A voice in the wilderness.

"Who are you?"
>That's what they asked Jesus.
>>"Are you an old one reappeared?"
>>"Are you a King, a leader of armies?"
>>"Are you a miracle-worker?"
>No, I am the Messiah,
>>God's presence — immortal.

"Who are you?"
>What if they asked me?
>>I am an American.
>>I am a parent — a child.
>>I am a worker.
>But am I also a Christian?
>>A seeker of the truth?
>>God's person?

Lord, forgive me my ambiguity —
>My unsureness of who I am,
>>What my mission is.
And give me the assurance of John,
>Of Jesus,
That I have a role in your plan.
>In Jesus' name I pray.
>>Amen

Advent 4

Luke 1:26-38

Christmas is here
    — Almost.
 And I'm ready for it
    — Almost.
    I'm prepared for the family celebration,
     Except for those few last-minute things,
   And I've tried to prepare for Christ.
I love Christmas —
    The trees and tinsel,
    The packages,
    The anticipation,
    The smells,
    The excitement,
      The Christmas Eve services,
        The candles,
        The carols.
It's always fresh.
  I'm like a child again,
     Filled with wonder.
But there's a sameness about it
      — I'm comfortable with,
      Comforted by,
       Tradition,
       The old carols,
      The familiar Scriptures.
I miss the radical nature
     Of the coming of Christ,
  Unexpected
    And unheralded.
Lord, forgive my jaded palate,
   My nesting myself in tradition,
       And surprise me again.
   Break into my life
      With the Christ Child,
       In whose name I pray.
         Amen

The Nativity of Our Lord
(Christmas Eve/Christmas Day)

Luke 2:1-20

An old story,
    A familiar story,
        A beloved story.
Jesus is born in a stable.
    The angels sing.
        The shepherds come to worship.
Tonight (today) I feel
    As if I were there!
    Hearing the music,
        Seeing the light
            — Marveling at the birth.
Because it's not just then and there;
    It's here and now.
    Jesus Is Born!
        The World Rejoices!
Lord, forgive me when I lose myself
    In "commercial Christmas."
    And remind me of the simplicity,
        The joy,
        The love
      Of that long-ago night (day)
  Which is also
    — For me —
  This Holy Night (Day).
        In Jesus' name I pray.
            Amen

New Year's Eve / Day

Luke 13:6-9

Made any good resolutions lately?
  It's a traditional New Year's activity —
    To list all the things we want to change,
        Hope to change,
    And resolve to do something about them.
  But even when they're taken seriously,
      Made with good intentions,
    They're soon broken,
      Forgotten,
        Thrown out with the noisemakers
          And party hats,
  Or at least put away for another year.
Made new resolutions?
    Of course not!
      I still have perfectly good ones left from last year.
Maybe that's why I don't make them —
    I don't intend to keep them,
        So why bother?
    I'm satisfied with myself the way I am —
      Imperfect,
        But lovable,
          Forgivable.
  (I don't want to be perfect anyway —
    I'm hard enough to put up with as I am!)
Lord, forgive my complacency,
    My too-easy satisfaction with myself,
    My too-ready excuse for my faults,
  And lead me to newness
      In my life,
        In my character,
    In Jesus Christ.
        Amen

Christmas 1 • The Holy Family (RC)

Luke 2:22-40

Wow!
    How did those two old people
        (Simeon and Anna)
            Know?
    Out of all the babies,
        All the families
    Who came to the temple,
        Day in,
            Day out,
    How did they know this one was special?
    How did they spot him?
And,
    More importantly
        (For me, anyway),
    How do *I* spot him
        Among all the people I see everyday?
They spent their lives watching,
        Waiting
        For God to break in,
            Announce his presence,
        And they saw him appear!
Can I do the same?
        Watch?
            Wait?
                And see my Lord?
Lord, forgive me when I lose heart,
        When I fail to look for you;
    And show me your presence
        In your people,
        In your world,
        In my heart.
    In Jesus' name I ask it.
            Amen

The Holy Name of Jesus

Luke 2:15-21

"Jesus,
    Jesus,
        Jesus,
There's something about that name!"
(So says the Gospel song.)
                There sure is!
        Not sappy sentimentality,
          Not "Jesusolotry,"
            Not an "expletive-deleted."
Power!

    That's what there is about it!
    It defines his mission
                — "Yahweh Saves,"
                    His name is Salvation!
  "In this sign we conquer."
    The "sign" is the Cross!
        The Cross bears the name of Salvation —
        J E S U S.
Lord, forgive me when I take your name
                For granted,
                  In vain,
And teach me the P O W E R
    Of your Name,
        The power to make me whole.
    I ask it in Jesus' Holy Name.
                Amen

Christmas 2

John 1:1-18

In the Beginning
    Was the Word!
        The Word of Creation,
        The Word of Life,
        The Word of Light,
        The Word that became flesh.
God has The Word;
        I have words.
    My words destroy —
        Words of criticism,
        Words of rejection.
    My words bring death —
        Words of hate,
        Words of fear.
    My words bring darkness —
        Words of confusion,
        Words of untruth.
    My words are set against
    GOD'S WORD.
Lord, forgive me when my words
        Ignore your Word,
        Cheapen it,
        Falsify it.
    And teach me the Word of Life,
        Even Jesus himself.
            Amen

The Epiphany of Our Lord
(January 6)

Matthew 2:1-12

Wise men and camels,
    Pageantry,
        Oriental mysticism,
    Beautiful
        — But what has it to do with me?
Like the rest of the Christmas story,
        It isolates the Christ from me!
            It's in a different time,
                A different space.
I know cars,
    Hospitals,
    Motels;
  Not camels,
    Magi,
    Stables.
I love the story.
    I wallow in the sentiment,
        The nostalgia.
Then I store it with the pageant costumes,
        The tree ornaments,
        For another year.
Maybe I need some contemporary "wise men,"
            Scientists,
                Unbelievers
        To point out the wonders
  That are right under my nose!
Lord, forgive my "familiarity that breeds contempt"
    (Or at least
        Bored repetition that precludes wonder),
    So that I too can see the star
            And follow it
        — Wondering —
            To Jesus.
            Amen

The Baptism of Our Lord
(Epiphany 1 • Ordinary Time 1)

Mark 1:4-11

"In those days Jesus . . . was baptized."
    How did they do it?
        Was he "dunked"?
            Immersed?
        Did he duck down
    While John watched?
    Did John pour water on him?
    Was he "sprinkled"?
I get so caught up in the mechanics —
    Infant or adult,
        "Christening" or "Believers,"
    Sprinkling,
        Pouring,
            Immersion,
Which words are said —
        That I forget what Baptism is all about!
For Jesus —
    An identification with humanity,
        With *Me;*
    An affirmation of who he was,
        What he was to do.
For me —
    A cleansing from sin,
    An assurance of grace,
        Forgiveness,
    An entry into the Body of Christ,
    A dedication to service.
Lord, forgive me for making your Sacrament
        A point of argument;
    And help me to accept your grace,
        Your commission,
    For myself,
    For my brothers and sisters in the faith,
        As Jesus did.
            Amen

Epiphany 2 • Ordinary Time 2

John 1:35-51

Come, follow me!
    Sure —
        Where are you going?
        How long will it take?
        When will we be back?
        Can I have time to get ready?
        What will it cost me?
When God calls
    I'm full of questions!
I've learned to be cautious,
    To be careful,
    To find out what's involved.
    I don't just jump into things blindly!
        That's a good way to get hurt!
But God's call doesn't come with guarantees!
        No pension plan,
        No Social Security,
        No insurance,
        No assurance of safety,
            Or even of success!
God calls me to be faithful,
    To commit myself
        Without question,
        Without reservation;
    And I'm afraid to respond!
Lord, forgive my fears
    For myself,
    For my family,
    For my future,
        And teach me to trust you
    Enough to follow
        Wholeheartedly,
    And for Jesus' sake.
        Amen

Epiphany 3 • Ordinary Time 3

Mark 1:14-20

How could they do that?
>Switch careers in midstream, as it were?
>>Go from "fisher folk"
>>To "fishers *for* folk"?

The symbolism is there,
>Especially if you like puns —
>>He increased their "net" profit (Prophets?)!
>>They were "hooked"!
>>They had a "line" on something good —
>>>The "reel" thing!

But what about the reality,
>The practicality?

What did they know about preaching,
>Teaching,
>Healing?

What about their responsibilities?
>Boats,
>Equipment,
>Employees,
>Families,
>Homes?

How could they just walk away
>To follow a glib-tongued stranger?

(What I really mean is . . .
>Could *I* do that?)

Lord, forgive me my fears,
>My excuses;
>>And teach me to follow Jesus,

Immediately
And
Faithfully,
>Wherever he leads.
>>Amen

Epiphany 4 • Ordinary Time 4

Mark 1:21-28

Authority!
>I have a problem with it!
>>With exercising it —
>>Who am I to tell you what to do?
>>>To say what's right or wrong
>>>>For someone
>>>>>else?
>>With accepting it —
>>Who are *you* to tell *me* what to do?
>I'm an adult.
>I'm responsible,
>>Moral,
>>Ethical.
>>>I don't need a boss!
I sometimes hesitate to give my opinion,
>>Much less demand my way.
>So I'm often disappointed,
>>Hurt,
>>Angry
>>>About group decisions.
If I have authority to back up my opinions,
>I ought to assert it!
And I often question the authority of others —
>Who do they think they are?
>"Who died and made you King?"
So I ignore it,
>Fight it,
>>And go my own way.
Lord, forgive my timidity
>And my resentment;
>>>Teach me to lead
>>>>And be led,
>Without fear or discontent,
According to your Word and will,
>>>And for Jesus' sake.
>>>>Amen

Epiphany 5 • Ordinary Time 5

Mark 1:29-39

What's all this talk about demons?
    It sounds like one of the things Jesus did most
                  Was cast out demons!
      That doesn't really fit my mind-picture.
           Teaching — yes.
           Preaching — sure.
           Healing — of course.
           But demons?
           Demons are outside my experience!
Physical disease is caused by germs
                Or viruses
                Or maybe genetics.
  Emotional/mental disease by environment,
                    Experiences,
                    Chemical imbalance
                        (Or maybe genetics).
    There's no room for Demons!
    They don't fit in my world!
But there are still things I,
         Doctors,
         Scientists
     Don't understand;
And I say
   I believe
       (sort of),
  Christ has power over them!
I *could* call them Demons
                (Maybe)!
Lord, forgive my intellectualizing,
     My refusal to credit what I don't understand,
           What doesn't fit my cosmology,
And cast out my personal Demons,
              Whatever I may call them.
    Free me to wholeness,
           For Jesus' sake
           And by his power.
                Amen

Epiphany 6 • Ordinary Time 6

Mark 1:40-45

The Miracles at Lourdes,
                      Oral Roberts,
                                    Faith-healers
        — Even Christian Scientists —
I'm skeptical!
    Many seem fraudulent
        Or psychosomatic
                Short-term cures
        — Maybe even dangerous —
        Hiding symptoms,
        Denying problems.
When I hear of people who depend on faith;
        Who refuse medicine,
        Doctors,
        Hospitals
    (Especially for their children);
Who cancel their health insurance;
                      I'm scornful,
                      Indignant.
    I want someone to intervene!
Does that mean I don't trust God
                As much as others do?
                As much as I should?
        Is it cynicism?
        Is it pride in human achievement?
        Is it lack of faith?
Lord, forgive me my human pride
    That says, "We know —
                Or can discover —
                      Everything!"
        And teach me that you are still in control
        Of your world
                And even of my body!
    I pray in Jesus' name.
                Amen

Epiphany 7 • Ordinary Time 7

Mark 2:1-12

I identify with the home owner.
    I've invited Jesus in
        And the crowd comes with him!
            Standing room only!
    I'm proud!
        The Master,
            The Healer,
                (The Messiah?),
                      In *my* house!
Then . . .
    A loud noise,
        Plaster falls,
            A big hole,
And a guy comes down on ropes
    Right through *my* ceiling!
"Who did that?"
        Who gave them permission?
        Who's going to fix it?
            (Am I covered for vandalism?
                Or is this a *real* Act of God?
                Wish I'd had a "Pru-Review"!)
I don't mind paying the price
    For *my* salvation.
    But why does *his* have to cost *me*?
    Lord, forgive me my selfishness,
        My cost-counting;
      And help me to lose myself
        In my neighbor's joy,
      And make it my own
        For his sake
      And mine
        And Jesus'.
            Amen

Epiphany 8 • Ordinary Time 8

Mark 2:18-22

New Wine,
    New ideas,
        A new spirit.
It sounds great!
        But it can be dangerous!
    Getting new
        Means giving up the old,
            The familiar,
            The comfortable,
    Sometimes even
           Destroying the old
— Bursting the old skins!
I want the new
    (I think),
    But I fear it
    If I have to change,
        Lose something I value.
      Maybe I'm better off not risking,
            Sticking to the old wine!
Lord, forgive me my unwillingness to change,
        To risk,
    And fill me with new wine.
            Burst my old skin
    And bring me to new life,
        For Jesus' sake.
            Amen

The Transfiguration of Our Lord

Mark 9:2-9

Peter had an Edifice Complex!
   Here he stood
       In the presence of mystery
  And his reaction is to build a shrine!
          To try to hang on to the moment,
            Capture it,
            Keep it,
         To make this the normative moment,
         To dwell in the past
              From now on.
But Jesus said "NO!"
     "Don't build *anything*!"
     "Don't even *tell* anybody about it!"
Remember the moment,
   Savor the experience,
But don't try to live there!
I'm like Peter.
   When I have a special moment,
       A vision,
           An experience of the Holy,
    I want to hang on to it;
    I want to live there,
      Build,
      Decorate;
         Show off my experience,
       Instead of going on toward the Kingdom.
Lord, forgive me my shortsightedness,
     My human desire to hold on to the moment,
  And help me to see glimpses of your glory
  And to look past them to the future
      And to your Kingdom,
           Jesus' Kingdom.
   I ask it in his name.
        Amen

Ash Wednesday

Matthew 6:1-6, 16-21

Ash Wednesday,
    The beginning of Lent —
        A season of sacrifice,
        A season of penitence.
    What shall I give up?
        Something I don't like
            Or can't do anyway?
        (Spinach?
            Playing pro-basketball?)
        Something that's not good for me?
        (Tobacco?
            Alcohol?)
        Something traditional?
        (Meat?)
And if I practice self-denial
        Who should I tell?
        Those who will help me?
        Those who will applaud me?
            (Those who will make fun of me?)
Or should my Lenten observation be private,
                Personal?
        "Not like the hypocrites"?
Or should it be more positive —
        Adding to, rather than taking away?
            More prayer,
            More Scripture reading,
            More acts of generosity,
            More expressions of love?
Lord, forgive me for not knowing how to observe Lent;
    And help me to use this season
        To come closer to you.
        Not just for six weeks,
            But forever.
        In Jesus' name,
            Who gave himself for me.
                Amen

Lent 1

Mark 1:9-15

"Lead us not into temptation."
   I don't need to be led —
                    I can find it easily by myself!
      Little temptations:
         "Eat another piece of candy."
         "Put that off till tomorrow."
         "Have another drink."
         "Forget it — it's not important."
      Bigger temptations:
         "Leave it to the experts" —
            Government to the politicians,
            Education to the teachers,
            Morality to the preachers.
     Temptations to cheat —
         At school,
         On the job,
         At tax time.
     Temptations to lie —
         When I don't want to do something,
            Or admit what I did do.
     Temptations to worship things instead of God —
         Popularity,
         Prestige,
         Power,
         Money.
I'm surrounded by temptation
    And it's so easy to give in!
Lord, forgive my lack of strength,
        Of Commitment;
   Help me to resist temptation
        And be faithful to you,
                  For Jesus' sake.
                        Amen

Lent 2

Mark 8:31-38

I love Peter!
    He's so human,
        So natural
            — So like me!
    He has flashes of insight
        — "You are the Christ!"
        Or visions
        — The Transfiguration.
    But he refuses to see the implications,
            The costs involved,
        And he backs away from what is to come.
    He can't accept that Jesus will die
        Or
            — More personally —
            That he will too!
I'm like that.
    I love Jesus;
        I look forward to God's Kingdom,
            But I'm not so sure about the Cross!
            That scares me!
        I'd rather forget that part altogether!
Lord, forgive me for only hearing the Good News
            And ignoring the bad.
    Help me to be realistic,
        To count the costs of discipleship,
            And to choose its joys
                Despite them,
        As Jesus did.
            Amen

Lent 3

John 2:13-25

Turning the tables —
        That was gutsy!
Disrupting business,
Confusing the count,
Destroying the merchandise,
Breaking tradition.
        Who did Jesus think he was, anyway?
I couldn't have done that!
    Imagine breaking up the Bazaar,
        Tripping over the ticket table,
        Crashing the crafts sale,
        Busting in on Bingo,
        Ripping the raffle tickets.
(But these are all part of the life of the church,
    And they are only occasional.
        They don't interfere with worship
            — Do they?)
These things aren't important;
    They're nothing to get upset over.
            And I don't!
(I don't get upset over important things either
    — About living out what I believe,
        Taking firm stands.)
Lord, forgive me for being so "wishy-washy"
            In my Christian life,
        For ignoring issues of ethics,
            Of right and wrong,
        For giving in to pressures of tradition
            Or public opinion.
Help me to know the right,
        The good,
        The true,
            And take my stand,
            Even if I stand alone
                As Jesus did.
                    Amen

Lent 4

John 3:14-21

I'm afraid of the dark!
                I stumble,
                I grope,
                I panic.
                I look for a flashlight,
                      A candle,
                      A match
                          — Anything
        So I can see my way.
Darkness is scary;
        It calls up the primitive in me —
                          The ancient fears.
But physical darkness,
                In itself,
                      Won't hurt me.
Spiritual darkness is something else!
           There too
                  I stumble,
                  I grope,
                  I panic.
                  I look for a light
                        — Anything to show the way.
Lord, forgive my stumbling,
       My fear,
               And teach me that Jesus is the light.
He takes away the darkness of my soul
    And guides my steps.
                    Let me follow him without fear.
                                     Amen

Lent 5

John 12:20-33

"Life — love it or lose it!"
      Sounds like a bumper sticker!
If we don't value
      Love,
            Ideals,
                  Freedom,
                        Democracy,
                              Justice,
                        Family,
                Church,
    Enough to protect them,
        They can slip away,
            Erode,
                Disappear without notice.
But Jesus put it another way:
    "Whoever loves his/her life, will lose it,
    Whoever hates life in this world will keep it
                        For eternity."
There's a switch,
        A paradox!
                (But it seems to work that way —
    My favorite shirt gets torn;
    The ugly one wears forever!)
Paradoxical statements make me think —
    There's truth in the slogans;
        I need to support what I value,
            But I can value things too much —
                Make idols of them,
                Worship them,
                Put them ahead of God.
                (And I do!)
Lord, forgive me my confusion
            Of mind,
            Of values;
And help me to realize that *nothing* else
        Is as important as your kingdom —
            Not my money,
            Not my politics,
                Not even my life.
I pray in the name of him who gave his life for me —
    Jesus, my Lord. Amen

Sunday of the Passion

Matthew 26:14 — 27:66
Mark 14:1 — 15:47

The Last Supper —
    Love
        And betrayal,
    Bread and Wine,
        Body and Blood,
    And silver.
        The sell-out.
I come to the Table.
    I dip my hand in the dish.
    I eat with,
        Partake of,
            My Lord,
  And I betray him!
        Oh, not like Judas,
        Not physically,
        Not personally.
    But in other ways:
  When my confessions of faith
    And my actions
        Don't coincide;
  When I don't live
    The faith I proclaim.
I, too, ask,
    "Is it I, Lord?"
        And he replies,
    "You have said so."
Lord, forgive my betrayals,
    My denials of you
        And your power to save me;
  Grant me the grace of your Sacraments
  And your power to repent,
        In Jesus' name,
    And for his sake.
        Amen

Palm Sunday
(When not observed as Sunday of the Passion)

Mark 11:1-11

Imagine:
    Two guys try to hot-wire my new convertible.
      "What are you doing to my car?"
        "The Lord needs it!"
    "Sure he does!"
    "Don't go away — I'm calling the police!"
It worked for the disciples —
    Nobody turned them in for being thieves!
I wonder how come.
    Did they know the owner?
    Were they too big to argue with?
    Were the bystanders afraid to get involved?
    Did they have an air of authority,
        Of righteousness?
I wouldn't mind helping out for a parade,
    But I'd need to be *asked*.
      Does God act that way?
        Politely say,
          "Would you please . . .
          Do you mind . . .
          If you have nothing better to do . . .?"
    Or does God assume
      My obedience,
      My acceptance,
      My agreement?
Lord, forgive my argumentative,
      Possessive
    Nature,
That which sets me up as supreme,
          As God;
And teach me to hear your call
      And to respond,
    Despite the cost,
        As Jesus did.
          Amen

Maundy Thursday

Mark 14:12-26
John 13:1-15

I like Mark's version of this night
  A lot better than John's!
    I get a special feeling
      About the Institution of the Sacrament,
        The closeness of the disciples,
        The lovely words of Jesus.
    I can wax nostalgic,
      Almost see myself there,
        Call it to memory each time I partake.
  But John!
    That footwashing scene —
      I sympathize with Peter!
        It's embarrassing!
        It's degrading!
        It's undignified!
    Can't I make my commitment to Christ
        And his service
      With dignity,
      With decorum?
    Do I have to be so
      Personal?
        So physical,
          About it?
Lord, forgive me for seeking the glory of your Kingdom,
      While avoiding the responsibilities;
  And help me to follow in Christ's footsteps —
    Personally,
      Physically,
        Really!
          For his sake,
  That of his people,
      And my own.
          Amen

Good Friday

John 18:1 – 19:42

What a terrible day!
   Terribly long,
      From shortly after midnight
                      To dark — or later.
   Terrible in its events:
      A frightening arrest,
         A personal betrayal,
            A mock trial,
               Physical abuse,
                   Political machinations,
                      A cruel death,
                          A hasty burial.
   Terrible in its implications —
      The death of hope,
         The death of God's own Son
            — The Spectre of death,
                      For
                        Me!
(If God suffers this way,
     What can a mere human expect?)
Even though I know the end
            (The beginning?)
                          Of the story,
   I still feel the despair
          Of
        Today!
Lord, forgive me when I try to live in my own Good Fridays;
   And give me the courage to come through them
      Whole,
      Confident in your Resurrection
                      And my own.
                          Amen

The Resurrection of Our Lord

Mark 16:1-8
John 20:1-18

An open door,
  An empty tomb,
    An angel in a white robe —
  A beautiful story!
    I believe it!
  (Especially at Easter!)
        Or perhaps,
          More honestly,
I suspend my disbelief!
  I do unusual things today:
    Color eggs,
    Eat candy,
    See bunnies and chicks,
    Wear new clothes,
        Go to church;
    Things I don't normally do.
      Why not pretend I believe?
  After all, I don't have to do anything about it!
Lord, forgive my disbelief,
  My preoccupation with myth,
  My play-acting;
And help me to see the reality behind the story,
    To meet the Risen Christ in my own garden,
    To know that my Redeemer lives,
    And that I too shall live,
          Forever.
            Amen

Easter 2

John 20:19-31

Thomas missed the Sunrise Service!
    (Sunset, if you want to be technical.)
  He wasn't with the others
      To see the Risen Christ,
          And he didn't believe them!
      He had to see,
        To touch
            For himself,
                So he could be sure.
I wasn't there either!
  I couldn't see for myself,
      Touch for myself,
      Satisfy myself
    That the Risen Lord
        Is the same as
      The One Who Died For Me.
            And so,
         Sometimes
            I wonder.
Lord, forgive my doubtings,
    My skepticism,
    My insistence on physical fact.
  And teach me to see with the eyes of faith,
    To say, with Thomas,
        "My Lord and My God!"
              Amen

Easter 3

Luke 24:35-49

Maybe if I'd been there —
    Saw Jesus,
        Touched him,
             Watched him eat,
        Heard him teach;
Maybe then it would be easier!
  I still don't know!
    I know the disciples
         Saw,
           Touched,
             Heard him
    (Or at least said they did).
  I know they believed
      And they convinced others.
  I know the church teaches that it happened,
      But I can't help wondering!
It's so foreign to my experience,
  So unusual,
    So . . .
      Impossible.
      I want to believe,
        But it's hard!
Lord, I believe —
    Help my unbelief!
  Give me assurance,
      And in the meantime,
  Help me to live in faith,
      About — and in
        Jesus, my Lord.
          Amen

Easter 4

John 10:11-18

"We're #1!"
    "Our team is best!"
        "Our country is best!"
            "Our church is best!"
    I get a little chauvinistic sometimes —
                      But that's okay.
    I should be proud of who I am,
                What I belong to.
        That's loyalty.
        That's patriotism.
        That's team spirit.
    The danger is
             When I deny that others —
                  Other teams,
                  Other towns,
                  Other nations,
                  Other churches —
        Have anything good about them!
        When the only way to make me feel good
        Is to make them look bad,
            To put them down.
    The Good Shepherd has other sheep,
            "Not of this fold"!
Lord, forgive me my chauvinism,
    The insecurity that keeps me from appreciating,
               From respecting,
                From honoring
        The beliefs,
        The commitments,
        The loyalties
            Of others;
    And help me to accept them
            As brothers and sisters
        In the love of Christ,
            In whose name I pray.
                Amen

Easter 5

John 15:1-8

Christ, you are the vine
        And I am a branch,
  Of little
     (Or no)
        Use, unless I bear fruit —
  Good,
     Plump,
        Juicy
           Grapes —
  Good to eat,
     Good for juice,
          Or jelly
             Or wine.
But when I produce at all,
         My "grapes" are often sour —
Discord,
     Dis-harmony,
        Jealousy —
Or else they're already raisins!
          Dried up,
       Withered,
     Hardened,
         Without the juice of life.
God, forgive my "crop failure,"
   My avoiding
      Or spoiling
         Your work in me;
And help me to bear good fruit,
    To be useful,
      Nourishing,
      Profitable
          For your work.
  I ask it in the name of the True Vine,
           Jesus, my Lord.
              Amen

Easter 6

John 15:9-17

I make my own choices!
                    I choose my friends.
                    I choose my work.
                    I choose where I will live.
                    I even choose my faith!
                        (At least, I think I do!)
Yet my choices are limited
    By geography,
        By economics,
            By birth,
                By ability,
                    By opportunity
    — Maybe by divine choices.
Jesus said,
    "You did *not* choose me —
                I chose *you!*"
    That makes me feel
           — I don't know —
        Manipulated?
          Dictated to?
          Not free?
I'm not sure I like it!
Lord, forgive my thoughtless claims of autonomy;
    And teach me to look for your plan,
        To accept your choice,
                And fulfil it.
      For Jesus' sake,
           Who chose me.
                Amen

Ascension Day/Ascension Sunday

           Luke 24:44-53
           Mark 16:15-20

Jesus was taken up into heaven!
    Hard to believe!
        Primitive Christianity!
    But I don't really care.
        What seems more important to me
           Is what he said before he went!
"Preach the Gospel to all people!"
        A commission for the Disciples
                        — And for me!
        (And one I don't carry out very well!)
    I say it's Good News,
           The best news ever!
        But I don't share it
           As I would a raise in salary,
                A windfall profit,
                A prize in the lottery,
                An honor given me
                        Or someone I love.
        (Maybe I assume everybody knows about it
            already.
        Maybe I don't want to seem strange,
                    Fanatic.
        Maybe I'm embarrassed about believing.)
I have a faith to proclaim,
    A Lord to love,
    A story to tell.
           Why do I hide who
                      And whose
                I am?
Lord, forgive me my reticence
    In proclaiming your Gospel;
    And help me
           To make disciples for Jesus
                Everywhere I go.
                      For his sake.
                            Amen

Easter 7

John 17:11-19

That they may be one!
    A prayer of Jesus,
        A dream of Christian unity.
    I'm not so sure I like it!
        I'm proud of what sets me apart,
                Sets my church apart!
    If "they are to be one,"
                Which one will "they" be?
    It's okay if all the churches want to join mine,
        But *not* so okay if I'm supposed to change,
                Give up what's important to me,
                Join theirs!
        And consider the practicality —
            The difficulty of agreeing on *anything*,
                Much less *everything!*
I hear it;
    I'll even pray for it,
            But I don't want to *do* it!
Lord, forgive my arrogant assumption
                That my way is the best
                (The only?)
                        Way;
And teach me your way
        Of unity in faith,
        In action,
        In love.
                For Jesus' sake
            — Who is One.
                Amen

The Day of Pentecost

John 16:5-15 (C)
John 7:37-39 (L)
John 20:19-23 (RC)

The Holy Spirit,
    The Holy Ghost,
        The Paraclete,
            The Comforter,
        Symbols of
            Dove,
                Wind,
                    Flame.
All of them somehow
        Ephemeral,
            Changing,
                Hard to hold
                — Or understand.
I don't really know what to do with The Spirit!
In the Old Testament —
    A gift of prophesy,
            Ecstatic utterance;
In the New Testament —
    A gift of tongues,
            Magic communications;
In some churches —
    Tongues,
        Healing,
            Visions,
                Unnatural
                    Other-worldly stuff.
What about for me?
    Do I have The Spirit?
            How can I know?
    (Especially when I don't do that stuff.)
Lord, forgive me my suspicion
            About the gifts
                And the powers Of your spirit.
    And dwell in me,
        Bringing me closer to you
      And to my Lord, Jesus the Christ. Amen

The Holy Trinity
(Common, Lutheran)

John 3:1-8

Born again!
    I hate that phrase!
        I wish Jesus hadn't used it!
            (Maybe he didn't —
                    Exactly —
              But the King James Version does!)
    It represents everything
             Extremist,
                  "Anti,"
                      Exclusive,
                  Prideful,
            Judgmental
                  In Christianity.
    It smacks of
        The Religious Right,
            The Moral Majority,
                The Fundamentalists,
  The TV preachers,
        The "Bumper-Sticker Bunch."
  I don't even want to think about it!
Lord, forgive me for judging other Christians
    By the language they use,
        And for letting other usages
                    Keep me from hearing
                        And keeping
            Any part of your Word.
    Let me experience Rebirth
            In your Spirit,
        That I may enter your Kingdom
                    Fresh,
                    Whole,
                    Pure.
            For Jesus' sake,
                And in his name.
                      Amen

The Holy Trinity
(Roman Catholic)

Matthew 28:16-20

"God in Three persons,
        Blessed Trinity!"
    What a confusing idea!
God is God,
      Jesus is God,
           The Holy Spirit is God;
     Jesus is not the Spirit,
  God is not Jesus —
     No wonder some people think Christians
             Have three Gods!
      I get confused myself!
       (So do other Christians!)
         Some worship Jesus almost
         exclusively;
        Some rely heavily
           (Solely/Soul-ly?)
              On the Spirit.
        Some see only the Creator;
     But we experience all three:
The Power of God,
    The Salvation of Christ,
       The Comfort of the Spirit,
         And still know that God is One!
Lord, forgive my preoccupation with doctrine,
         With defining,
           Pigeonholing
              You.
And let me experience your love
        In every way,
     As I have need.
   In the name of the Creator,
      The Christ,
         And the Holy Spirit.
            Amen

Usage Guide for the Sundays After Pentecost

The three lectionaries which the prayers in this book serve locate them differently in the second half of the church year, the Sundays after the Day of Pentecost. The Lutheran lectionary assigns the prayers according to the Sundays after Pentecost. The Pentecost designations which appear in the pages which follow refer to the Lutheran lectionary.

Denominations using the Common lectionary also refer to Sundays in the second half of the church year as Sundays "after Pentecost," but the Scripture texts (and hence the prayers) in this half of the church year are assigned not to Sundays after Pentecost per se, but rather to fixed dates. The Roman Catholic lectionary, which uses the terminology "Sundays in Ordinary Time" during this second half of the church year, also follows this fixed-date system for the assignment of texts. The following chart will indicate the scheme according to which the texts and prayers are assigned:

Common Lectionary	Roman Catholic Lectionary	Fixed-date Assignment
Proper 4	Ordinary Time 9	May 29 — June 4
Proper 5	Ordinary Time 10	June 5-11
Proper 6	Ordinary Time 11	June 12-18
Proper 7	Ordinary Time 12	June 19-25
Proper 8	Ordinary Time 13	June 26 — July 2
Proper 9	Ordinary Time 14	July 3-9
Proper 10	Ordinary Time 15	July 10-16
Proper 11	Ordinary Time 16	July 17-23
Proper 12	Ordinary Time 17	July 24-30
Proper 13	Ordinary Time 18	July 31 — August 6
Proper 14	Ordinary Time 19	August 7-13
Proper 15	Ordinary Time 20	August 14-20
Proper 16	Ordinary Time 21	August 21-27
Proper 17	Ordinary Time 22	August 28 — September 3
Proper 18	Ordinary Time 23	September 4-10
Proper 19	Ordinary Time 24	September 11-17
Proper 20	Ordinary Time 25	September 18-24

Common Lectionary	Roman Catholic Lectionary	Fixed Date Assignment
Proper 21	Ordinary Time 26	September 25 — October 1
Proper 22	Ordinary Time 27	October 2-8
Proper 23	Ordinary Time 28	October 9-15
Proper 24	Ordinary Time 29	October 16-22
Proper 25	Ordinary Time 30	October 25-29
Proper 26*	Ordinary Time 31**	October 30 — November 5
Proper 27	Ordinary Time 32	November 6-12
Proper 28	Ordinary Time 33	November 13-19
Christ the King	Christ the King	November 20-26

* The Sunday nearest November 1 may be observed as All Saints' Sunday
** When November 1 is a Sunday it is observed as All Saints' Sunday

Proper 4 • Pentecost 2 • Ordinary Time 9
Mark 2:23 – 3:6

"Remember the sabbath day,
        To keep it holy!"
I do —
    Remember, that is!
        I go to church,
            Usually,
                If nothing else comes up!
    I rest,
        Kind of,
            Unless I have to work!
I'm just not fanatical about it!
    After all, didn't Jesus say,
        "The sabbath is made for people,
            Not people for the sabbath"?
What's important about the sabbath anyway?
    Keeping the seventh day
        (Or in my case, the first day) Clear?
        Or making time for myself —
            Time to reflect,
            Time to worship,
            Time to get myself together?
    (Whoops!
        Trapped again!
            I don't even do that well!)
I fill all my days
    With busyness,
        Work, and play.
I don't take — or make —
    Time for worship,
        Reflection,
        Meditation;
            And I lose by it.
Not just by ignoring one of the "Big 10,"
    But by not letting myself be re-created.
Lord, forgive me for thinking
        I make the world spin;
    And teach me to rest,
        To keep your sabbath.
    For your sake
        And my own. Amen

Proper 5 • Pentecost 3 • Ordinary Time 10

Mark 3:20-35

A Kingdom divided,
    A family divided
             Cannot stand!
    Clear,
        Logical,
            True.
                But like many truths,
        Easier said than acted on!
I value the nation,
    The family,
            — The church.
I want to see them whole and strong.
    But there is so much division —
        Civil wars and rebellions,
        Broken homes,
        Split churches —
    Because people hold different positions,
        And can't
            (or won't)
        Compromise.
Should I hold what I believe,
            "Through hell and high water,"
        To the point of schism?
Or should I compromise my convictions
    For the sake of unity?
        Or is there another way?
Lord, forgive my indecisiveness,
    My giving up what I should hold firm,
    My stubbornness when I should compromise;
And teach me your way,
    The way to strength
             Through submission
        To your will,
    Shown in Jesus, my Lord.
            Amen

Proper 6 • Pentecost 4 • Ordinary Time 11

Mark 4:26-34

Jesus was a right brain person!
    He spoke in metaphors,
        Parables,
        Similies.
    "The Kingdom is like a Mustard Seed."
        Why didn't he say it straight out?
Give me the rules,
    The structures,
    The formula for being Christian?
    (I'm more left brain —
            I can't really help it —
        My culture demands it,
            Values it.)
    I need structure,
        Organization,
        Efficiency.
            But that makes it hard
                To understand Jesus,
                To put myself in his shoes
                    (well, sandals),
                To be what he calls me to
                be.
Lord, forgive my arrogance,
    My trying to superimpose
My needs,
My organization,
My structure,
        On your Word.
And help me to hear,
    To grasp
        What is not understandable,
            Except by your grace.
    In his name I ask it.
        Amen

Proper 7 • Pentecost 5 • Ordinary Time 12

Mark 4:35-41

"Why are you afraid?"
                       That's a stupid question!
      Here are the disciples
               In a small boat,
               In a storm,
           And Jesus asks,
                  "Why are you afraid?"
     You'd have to be crazy not to be afraid!
Why am I afraid?
                 That's a dumb question, too!
        Look at my world!
                 Filled with dangers —
           From nuclear holocaust
                    To economic ruin
               To personal injury
                    To malicious mischief.

     So many things affect me —
        Most of them out of my control —
           I'd have to be nuts not to be afraid!
              Anyone with sense would be —
                           is!
(Not petrified —
      Not unable to live
               Or act,
        But
           afraid!)
Lord, forgive me my fears,
          My wish to control everything,
          My valuing safety above all;
    And teach me to accept,
        To know
              That you know,
And that nothing can separate me from you,
      Or from my Lord, Jesus,
            In whose name I pray. Amen

Proper 8 • Pentecost 6 • Ordinary Time 13

2 Samuel 6:1-15
Mark 5:21-43

Touch the Ark and die!
        Pretty severe action!
    Especially for someone who was just trying to help!
      No wonder King David was afraid!
        ("Indiana Jones" had the same problem!)
Touch Jesus and live!
        Pretty powerful person!
   Some difference!
      (Of course, it took faith —
          Absolute trust in the power of Christ,
          Complete assurance of his divinity.)
  I fear touch,
      Not of the Ark,
      But of people,
          And of God!
  If you get too close
        To emotions,
        To hurts,
        To the real stuff of life;
  If you let yourself be touched
        You can get hurt!
    So I keep my distance;
          I don't open myself to people.
      I don't let them get inside me
         Or get inside them,
       Lest I die,
          At least a little,
           From their pain.
Lord, forgive my fear of touching
          And being touched
           In any real way;
  And open me to be touched to the heart
           By you
          And your people,
    That I may be healed by the power of Christ,
          In whose name I pray. Amen

Proper 9 • Pentecost 7 • Ordinary Time 14

Mark 6:1-6

"Jesus could do no mighty work there."
                                              That's strange!
                                              Weird!
                                              Almost unbelievable!
       Because the hometown folks knew him,
       Because they knew his family
              They put him in a box!
              They didn't believe he was special,
                       So,
                            To them,
                       He wasn't!
How about here and now?
    Why don't I see miracles?
            Mighty works?
  Could it be for the same reason?
     Have I put Jesus in a box?
           To bring out and admire on Sunday?
           To ignore the rest of the time?
      Have I limited Christ
                To a teacher?
                A miracle worker?
                An historical figure?
    And so kept him from being
              My Lord
                    Here and now?
Lord, forgive my lack of vision,
    My lack of faith;
  And help me to see the Christ as he is —
          All powerful,
       Not limited by my faith
                Or lack of it.
      For his sake,
           And mine.
              Amen

Proper 10 • Pentecost 8 • Ordinary Time 15

Mark 6:7-13

Vacation time!
    When I pack for a week or two
        I've got enough stuff to set up house!
            Food,
            Clothing,
            Recreational equipment,
            Toys and games,
            Tools,
                Some "just in case" supplies.
        I always have lots I don't need
            And forget something necessary!
        I try to anticipate,
            To be prepared for anything.
When Jesus sent out the disciples,
    (Not on vacation, but to work)
        He said, "Don't take anything!"
            No food,
            No money,
                Not even an overnight case!
    Trust those whom you will serve.
    Trust God for your needs.
                I couldn't do that!
        I'd be afraid of not having what I needed.
        I'd be ashamed of asking for help.
If that's what it takes,
            I wouldn't make a good disciple!
Lord, forgive my fears,
    My illusions of self-sufficiency;
And teach me to depend on you
            (Not so much for my physical needs,
            But for the needs of my spirit);
And give me the assurance that you will provide,
                For Jesus' sake.
                      Amen

Proper 11 • Pentecost 9 • Ordinary Time 16

Mark 6:30-34

People,
 "Like sheep without a shepherd,"
  Looking for something
            — Anything —
     To give direction,
      Meaning
        To life.
                It's tragic.
I see people following all kinds of movements —
Exercise programs,
   Diet fads,
      TV preachers,
         Cultic groups —
    Trying to find direction,
          Meaning,
           Perfection;
  And so often
         Going from one
                To
                  Another,
      Never finding what they need,
Always wandering
           lost
           and
           alone
   (And sometimes
         I
            Do
              Too.)
Lord, forgive my frantic searching for "something,"
              "Someone"
                      To guide me;
    And bring me back to you,
         The true Shepherd.
                        Amen

Proper 12 • Pentecost 10 • Ordinary Time 17

John 6:1-15

Five dinner rolls
          And two little fish
                    To feed 5,000 people?
    You've got to be kidding!
              What *really* happened
                    Must have been shame.
      Jesus held the little boy's lunch up
      And people were shamed
             Into sharing what *they* had brought.
A sandwich here,
                    A candy bar there,
          Over yonder, a whole picnic basket,
                    Right?
Wrong!
    We're talking miracles here,
              Not logic!
              Not rationalization!
        (Maybe,
            — Perish the thought —
              Not even history!)
The message
      — Hard as it is to hear —
  Is that Jesus is enough
              For all my needs!
Lord, forgive me for listening only with my ears,
      For understanding only with my mind;
  And teach me to listen with my heart,
        To understand in my soul,
      For that is where you speak to me,
            Through Jesus, my Lord.
                    Amen

Proper 13 • Pentecost 11 • Ordinary Time 18

John 6:24-35

"I am the Bread of Life."
           Eat it and never hunger again.
  Wouldn't it be wonderful?
         Never to be hungry?
     (Think what you'd save on groceries!)
   A great scientific advance,
       The answer to the world's problems;
But, of course,
      That's not what he meant!
  Food is a problem for the world —
          Production,
            Distribution;
    But the *real* problem
        Is spiritual!
          That's *my* problem, anyway!
    I have enough to eat,
       More than enough;
  But my spirit often comes near starvation.
    I eat the bread of death,
     Not the Bread of Life;
    I drink the waters of destruction,
     Not the Living Water;
         And I perish
  In the midst of fatness.
Lord, forgive my preoccupation with the physical,
  And give me the Bread of Life,
    The Living Water,
         That my soul may thrive
         For Jesus' sake.
           Amen

Proper 14 • Pentecost 12 • Ordinary Time 19

John 6:35, 41-51

"Hey, we know this guy!
   We know his parents
      His history!
            How can he be anything special?"
   Familiarity *does* breed contempt!
      I know it.
      I see it all the time
         — How people are judged by their families,
              By the past.
"That's one of the Smith boys
            — None of them are any good!"
"Don't have anything to do with the Jones girl
            — She's trouble!
            They all are!"
It's not surprising that neighbors saw Jesus like that.
   "Who does he think he is, anyway?
      He's putting on airs,
         Trying to be something he's not!"
   But he *was!*
      He *is!*
         And they didn't,
            Couldn't
              See it!
Lord, forgive me my prejudice,
   My pre-judging
      People,
         Events
            — Even you;
And teach me to see what is,
        Instead of what I think ought to be.
     In Jesus' name
          — Who was also judged.
              Amen

Proper 15 • Penteocst 13 • Ordinary Time 20

John 6:51-58

"Eat my flesh — Drink my blood!"
                                  That's terrible.
    That's cannibalism!
                It's illegal,
                Immoral,
                Sickening.
      I hear the words so often
                I gloss over them.
I "pretty them up."
                    I spiritualize them
        So much that I lose sight of the scandal.
Jesus wasn't talking pretty
                  "Religious talk,"
                  Pious platitudes.
He meant it for *real* —
                Broken body,
                Spilled blood,
                        Sacrifice.
He gave his life
            For me,
                For you.
He didn't symbolize it.
    He didn't suggest it.
                      He *did* it!
Lord, forgive me for taking you too lightly,
        For being so nicely religious
                That I forget what you really did,
    And what you call me to do —
            Give myself for others,
                          As Jesus did.
                                      Amen

Proper 16 • Pentecost 14 • Ordinary Time 21

John 6:55-69

It's too hard!
    Following Jesus,
        Taking him seriously
    Was too hard for some of the disciples.
      They heard what he wanted from them.
      They got discouraged.
        They went home;
    And they knew him personally,
        Physically!
It's hard for me,
    Maybe too hard!
  Take up my cross,
      Give up my life,
  Go against my culture,
    My community,
    My family,
      All for the sake of him.
  Who does he think I am?
    (Maybe better,
      Who do *I* think *he* is?)
It's hard,
  But as Peter said,
    "What choice is there?
    Who else has the words of eternal life?"
Lord, forgive my fears,
  My lack of confidence
      In myself,
        And in you;
And give me strength to follow
    Where Jesus leads.
      In his name I pray.
        Amen

Proper 17 • Pentecost 15 • Ordinary Time 22

Mark 7:1-8, 14-15, 21-23

Ritual!
    It's important to do things
        "Decently and in good order"!
            To worship properly,
                Sing the right responses,
                Recite the proper creeds,
                Celebrate the Sacraments
                      With the appropriate words,
                          The proper gestures.
    But sometimes
        Ritual
            Becomes more important than
                Reality!
            Reading the right version
                Is more important
                    Than reading
                          Scripture!
            Worshiping in the proper form
                Is more important
                    Than worshiping
                          God!

    I forget that ritual
        Tradition,
    Are important
            Not for themselves,
    But for what they point to
                — GOD!
Lord, forgive me for my hypocrisy,
        For being more concerned with appearances
                Than with reality;
    And give me a clean heart,
            For Jesus' sake.
                Amen

Proper 18 • Pentecost 16 • Ordinary Time 23

Mark 7:31-37

"He makes the deaf to hear
    And the dumb to speak!"
       I'm deaf!
           Not physically —
    But I only hear what I want to hear,
        What agrees with my preconceptions,
            My prejudices.
    I don't hear the cries of people in pain.
    I don't even hear the Good News!
And I'm dumb.
      I can speak,
    But my speech is so often
           Idle,
              Inconsequential.
    I don't speak the word of truth.
    I don't tell the Good News!
Lord, forgive my deafness,
    My dumbness,
        Not physical
   But spiritual,
    Willful.
Open my ears that I may hear.
Open my mouth that I may speak
          The Good News,
       Of Jesus, my Lord.
            Amen

Proper 19 • Pentecost 17 • Ordinary Time 24

Mark 8:27-38

Who do people say Jesus is?
    Lots of things!
        A prophet,
        A holy man,
        An historical figure,
        A miracle worker,
        A divine messenger,
        A moral teacher,
        An exceptionally good person,
        A cult founder,
        A mystical healer.
Who do I say Jesus is?
    I say
        — With Peter —
    The Christ of God,
    My Lord and my Savior!
But I'm not always sure
        What I mean by that!
I treat Jesus like other people do —
        As an object of veneration,
        As a famous person in history,
        As a target for prayer,
        As an example for living.
But do I really treat him
    As living Lord?
        As my Master?
Sometimes
    I
      wonder!
Lord, forgive my confusion,
    My lack of faith;
And teach me that to know my Lord
    Is more important than
        Defining him!
    In Jesus' name
        (And despite my confusion).
            Amen

Proper 20 • Pentecost 18 • Ordinary Time 25

Mark 9:30-37

Lord, the world often seems upside-down to me.
    The good people suffer
        While the unrighteous prosper.
    Folks who have done only good
      (At least as far as I know)
        Feel excruciating pain:
        Physically — their bodies deteriorate with age or disease,
          Their minds wander with senility;
        Emotionally — they lose loved ones,
          Their hopes are dashed.
          While some who make a career out of evil,
      Who lie and cheat and steal and even kill,
    Never seem to have a twinge of conscience
          Or a pang of loss
          Or a problem in the world.
Why is it that when I try to follow you
    I don't seem to get the reward I deserve?
        Am I doing something wrong?
        Am I deluding myself about my righteousness?
        Or do I just misunderstand the rules?
Lord, forgive my petty concerns with myself,
          With my rewards,
          With my due;
And help me to turn the world upside-down
          In another way —
    To value love,
        Compassion,
       Truth,
       Purity,
          More than wealth and power and fame.
    For Jesus' sake
        And my own.
          Amen

Proper 21 • Pentecost 19 • Ordinary Time 26

Mark 9:38-50

Lord, I don't trust people.
   I don't trust the Russians
      Or the Israelis
         Or the PLO
            Or even our own government!
   I don't trust the neighbors.
      I keep my doors locked
         (Or if I'm gone, set up a timer on the lights).
   I think about getting a burglar alarm.
   I expect people to cheat me,
      To lie to me,
      To shortchange me,
      Not to do what they promise to do
         When they promise it.
   I don't trust other Christians,
         Other churches.
   I expect them to be "just like everybody else,"
      To be concerned with their own well-being
      And not to respect me or mine.
   Sometimes I don't even trust *you!*
      (I know I should, but I'm so used to relying on myself,
      And myself alone.)
Lord, forgive me my suspicions
      (And especially those which are self-fulfilling —
      Those people who react negatively
         Because I treat them negatively).
   Help me to develop a loving trust of others
      And of *you* —
   One which doesn't lay me open to injury,
   But which gives others the benefit of my doubt.
   And let me walk with you in perfect trust,
      As Jesus did.
         Amen

Proper 22 • Pentecost 20 • Ordinary Time 27

Mark 10:2-16

I want to be me!
        Free,
            Responsible,
                Independent,
                    Strong.
    I want to stand alone!
        To fight the world — and win!
        To be looked up to,
        To be depended on.
    But I also want to be taken care of —
            Coddled,
                Protected,
                    Insulated from the cold, cruel world.
I want to do!
    I want to be done for.
I want to protect!
    I want to be protected.
Independent —
    Dependent.
A decision-maker —
    Have decisions made for me.
Lord, I'm confused!
    Forgive me my indecision,
        My fears of dependence;
    And help me to come to wholeness,
        To relationships of giving and taking,
            Of interdependence
        With spouse or friend
            And with you.
                For Jesus' sake.
                    Amen

Proper 23 • Pentecost 21 • Ordinary Time 28

Mark 10:17-30

It's impossible!
    I can't do it!
No matter how hard I try,
    I can't be perfect!
    I read the Scriptures
        And hear the call to perfect obedience.
            "Follow all of the law."
            "Sell everything you have."
            "Be born again."
            "Don't even *think* evil."
And I can't do it!
        I have needs —
    Basic needs
        Like food, clothing, shelter.
    Security needs
        Like a job and money in the bank.
    Comfort needs
        Like nice things and an occasional luxury.
And I have responsibilities —
        To family,
        To employers,
        To my church and my community.
I can't meet my responsibilities to self and people
    And follow the hard lines of the Gospel.
        (Some things are just impossible —
        Like a camel through a needle's eye,
        Or a 727 in a one-car garage!)
If I have to give up everything to follow Jesus,
    I guess I lose!
Lord, forgive me for my lack of commitment,
    And let me know your grace
        That gives me what I can't earn
            (And don't deserve)
        — Your love and acceptance —
            Not for my own sake,
            But for Jesus'.
                    Amen.

Proper 24 • Pentecost 22 • Ordinary Time 29
Mark 10:35-45

Power!
    Authority!
        And the "perks" that go with it!
I want it!
I want my ability,
    My superiority,
        To be recognized
        And rewarded!
And I'm willing to do
    Whatever I need to do
        To get it!
I'm ambitious!
    I'm self-confident!
        I'm strong!
I need it!
    (If I can't get it in the world
    I'll take it in the church!)
But Jesus says true power,
    True leadership,
        Come through service,
        Through giving
        Instead of taking.
(I don't think my world works that way —
    If I don't blow my own horn
    Nobody else will!
How can I get what I want
    If I don't ask
        And work
    For it?)
Lord, forgive my human,
    Worldly,
        Perspective,
        Values;
And teach me the ways of your Kingdom
    — To seek
        Not to be first,
        But to serve,
            As Jesus did. Amen.

Proper 25 • Pentecost 23 • Ordinary Time 30

Mark 10:46-52

I want to see again!
    Oh, I'm not physically blind
                      But I wear "blinders"!
        My vision is narrow,
            Constricted,
            Limited,
        By my social class,
            My church affiliation,
            My economic status,
            My occupation,
            My nationality,
            My race.
I don't see the beauty of God's creation
    — I'm too busy driving through it.
I don't see God's people
    — I'm too focused on me.
I don't even see my own family,
    — I'm too busy taking care of them!
Jesus, Son of David, have mercy on me!
    Let me see anew,
        Freshly,
        Completely.
                Take off my blinders.
                Open my eyes.
Lord, forgive my willful blindness,
        My refusal to see;
    And open my eyes
                To your creation
                      And your Kingdom,
                For Jesus' sake.
                      Amen

Proper 26 • Pentecost 24 • Ordinary Time 31
Mark 12:28-34

Do I wear my faith on my sleeve
   Or hide it in my pocket?
      I know people who seem to say,
"If you've got it, flaunt it!"
          Who wear big crosses,
            Whose cars have Christian bumper stickers,
            Who are full of "Jesus talk,"
(But who often make me uncomfortable).
      So I am more likely to hide my faith,
        Not to offer my church affiliation,
        Not to seem "better than anyone else"
           (That's "holier than thou" in common language!),
        Not to appear different or strange:
   And I wonder:
            Am I being faithful?
            Am I denying my Lord?
            Am I ashamed of him?
            Can I be his servant?
            Can I "stand up for Jesus"
              And still be one of the gang?
        Is there a middle ground
   Between,
      On the one hand,
           "Pernicious Piety"
      And, on the other hand,
           Silent membership?
Lord, forgive me my fears
        Of being different,
        Of being thought strange,
        Or "too religious."
Grant me the courage to speak out
And the wisdom to know how
          And when;
    For the sake of him whom I pledged to serve,
      Jesus Christ, my Lord and my Savior.
                Amen

Proper 27 • Pentecost 25 • Ordinary Time 32

Mark 12:38-44

Easy for her!
    If you haven't got enough
        To do *anything,*
      Why not give it away?
  But me —
    Let's not be foolish!
      I give
        To church,
        To charity
          Of course!
        As much as I can spare
          (Sometimes a little more)!
  But I have responsibilities —
    Family,
    Bills
      — A credit rating to consider.
  I have to meet my obligations
        first!
Don't talk to me
  About little old ladies
      With their pennies!
Lord, forgive my penny-pinching,
    Cost-counting,
    Grudging giving;
And teach me to share like the widow,
  Not from my surplus,
    But of my substance,
        Trusting in you,
          For Jesus' sake.
            Amen

Proper 28* • Pentecost 26 • Ordinary Time 31**

Mark 13:1-13
(Mark 13:24-32 — See Pentecost 27)

"Don't let anyone fool you!"
    Easier said than done!
        So many things clamor for my attention,
            My loyalty;
            Claim to give me security
            And hope —
        Politicians who promise the moon and stars;
        The Pentagon promises an unshakable defense;
        Banks promise to make me a millionaire;
            (IRAs for a secure future)
        Companies "building for tomorrow" with my
            assets.
I want to trust,
    To believe,
    To be safe.
           But the Gospel tells me
        They are not in charge
        And neither am *I!*
                      God is!
How can I trust God
        Through turmoil,
            Terror,
    And still live
        In *this* world?
Lord, forgive my fears and confusion,
    My trust in false idols;
And teach me to trust in you,
            Always
                And only.
                    Amen

* Proper 26 may be replaced with All Saints' Sunday
** When Ordinary Time 31 falls on 1 November it is observed as All Saints' Sunday

Pentecost 27
(Lutheran Only)

Mark 13:24-31

The end of the world!
        Part of me fears it —
            Military holocaust,
            Nuclear winter,
            Political upheaval,
            Economic collapse,
              Even conventional warfare,
  Or natural
      (Semi-natural?)
              Disaster;
      A cosmic collison,
        Climactic changes,
        Mass famine,
          Earthquake,
          Flood,
            Fire.
The world,
      Physical
          Or human,
  Is so fragile,
  So carefully balanced,
            That it's scary!
Part of me doesn't believe it
            (That the world will end);
      Not in my lifetime,
      Not even in my wildest dreams!
  That's for pessimists
      Or religious fanatics!
Lord, forgive both my fear
    Of that which I cannot control,
    And my complacency
    That denies human responsibility;
And help me to live in the knowledge
    Of your power
      And your care.
           In the love of Jesus.
                Amen

Christ the King

John 18:33-37

Christ the King!
    I don't know what to do with that!
        We don't have a King;
        We don't *want* one!
            (We fought a war to get *rid* of one!)
    Kings
        If they're not just figureheads —
        Have too much power,
           Too much authority —
    They're dictators!
             And that's un-American!
    Kings are out of date anyway!
        I can try to weasel out of it
           — Christ's Kingdom is not of this world.
But if it is a *real* Kingdom
    He demands *total* allegiance,
    He wields *total* power,
        And I'm *totally* subject to him.
           He *owns* me —
                Body,
                Mind,
                And Spirit.
I'm not sure I can affirm that!
    (Honestly,
        I'm pretty sure,
            I *can't!*)
Lord, forgive my rebellion against your rule,
    And help me to accept you
           As my Lord
                And my King,
        Forever and ever.
            Amen

Reformation Sunday

(Last Sunday in October, Lutheran)

John 8:31-36

Reformed,
    Improved!
        Re-Formed,
           Made Over!
Reformation,
    Re-Formation!
        Whatever it is, I need it!
I try to save myself by being good,
        By doing good;
But all I see is how poorly I do!
I could always do better
    If I tried harder,
    If I wanted to more,
    If I could keep my promises
        To my friends and family,
        To myself,
           To you!
I need to be re-formed, made-over!
    A new creation, in the image of Christ!
Lord, forgive me those good intentions
    That somehow don't become actions,
    And accept me as I am —
        Imperfect,
           Unworthy,
                Poor and humble,
    (Or rich and arrogant).
By your grace — and for the sake of your Son, Jesus.
                            Amen

All Saints' Sunday • All Saints' Day
(First Sunday in November • November 1)

John 11:32-44
Matthew 5:1-12

Who's a Saint?
    Traditionally,
        The Great
        Holy
        People of the Faith.
    The ones who performed mighty works
        Before
            — Or after —
                Their death.
    For (Saint) Paul,
        The members of Christian congregations,
        Those saved by faith.
    In popular speech,
        Good people,
            Those who never complain
                No matter what the provocation.
    Archaic language?
    Maybe.
But admirable,
    Honorable,
    Worth striving for!
Lord, forgive my lack of saintliness,
    My obsession with me
            And mine,
        Instead of with you
            And yours;
    And lead me toward sainthood
        In my life,
            Both temporal
                And spiritual.
            For Jesus' sake.
                Amen

Thanksgiving Eve/Day

Luke 17:11-19

Thanksgiving!
    Turkey and football,
        Friends and relatives,
            Parades and "groaning boards"
                (Indigestion and sugar hangovers!).
    An American tradition!
        Pilgrims and Indians,
            The Mayflower and all that.
                A time of personal thanksgiving —
                    For a day off from work or school,
                    For the blessings of abundance,
                    For too much food and drink.
        (But holidays can be a bummer!
            Too much togetherness,
            Too little activity.
                We get on each other's nerves!
Kids underfoot,
    Everybody "housebound."
                        Maybe family is better
                        Taken in small doses!)
    Sometimes we "celebrate" because we're supposed to,
                Instead of because we want to;
        And our celebration is empty and meaningless,
            Even destructive of people
                And of souls!
Lord, forgive our ungratefulness
        For life,
        For abundance,
        For love,
            For your salvation;
    And teach us to be truly thankful,
            To really give thanks at Thanksgiving
        And through all of life.
We ask it in the name of Jesus,
            For whose presence we are *truly* thankful.
                      Amen